GOURMET CUISINE
Island Style

by MICHAEL GALLAGHER

ISLAND PLANTATIONS
™

Published and distributed by

 ISLAND HERITAGE
P · U · B · L · I · S · H · I · N · G

94-411 KŌʻAKI STREET, WAIPAHU, HAWAIʻI 96797

ORDERS: (800) 468-2800

INFORMATION: (808) 564-8800

FAX: (808) 564-8877

islandheritage.com

ISBN# : 0-89610-654-3

First Edition, First Printing - 2003

Photographer: Roméo S. Collado

Food Stylist: Nina Pfaffenbach

Introduction

Hawaiʻi is an island paradise for its beautiful scenery and its delicious food. Nowhere else in the world can you find the wide assortment of fresh foods from the land and ocean that make for exciting innovative culinary creations. Add to that the unique ethnic diversity of the islands' population originating from Asia, Europe, America and the South Pacific, and you have a distinctive cuisine found nowhere else in the world.

Hawaiʻi chefs are especially fond of using fresh tropical fruits in their cooking. The flavors of these fruits are preserved in products that are easy to use in creating the delicious foods of paradise.

~ ABOUT THE CHEF ~

Michael Gallagher is the executive chef of the award winning *Sea House* restaurant at the *Nāpili Kai Beach Resort* on the island of Maui. Born and raised on the New Jersey shore, he has over 20 years of culinary experience. Using the bounty of Hawaiʻi's land and sea, Chef Gallagher fuses the cuisine of his New England background with the flavors of Asia, Europe and Hawaiʻi, inventing wonderful flavor combinations that are exciting, fresh and delicious!

TABLE OF CONTENTS

Appetizers and Hearty Snacks

Salads and Light Entrees

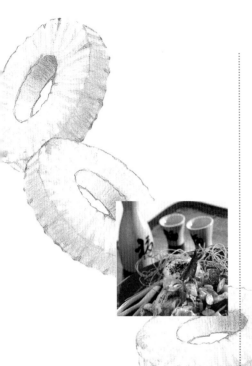

Seafood and Fish

Meat and Poultry

Sweet Beginnings and Endings

Shrimp Lumpia with Pohā Chili Dipping Sauce

Appetizers and Hearty Snacks

Melon-Wrapped Prosciutto with Toasted Maui Onion Vinaigrette

Ripe melon wrapped in cured ham is a classic of the Italian table. Embellished with vinaigrette flavored with toasted Maui onions, this fresh approach is even better. **Serves 12**

Cut cantaloupe and honeydew wedges in half. Cut prosciutto slices in half. Wrap prosciutto around melon pieces and arrange on a serving platter.

In a blender, place the mustard, vinegar and garlic and blend on high speed until smooth, about 30 seconds. Slowly add the oil and blend until well mixed. Season to taste with salt and pepper. Drizzle vinaigrette over the prosciutto wrapped melon. Garnish with mint and serve.

To roast garlic cloves: Cut about ¼ off the top of a bulb of garlic. Place in a shallow ovenproof dish. Drizzle with 3 to 4 tablespoons olive oil. Cover with foil and bake in a 300°F oven for about 45 minutes or until garlic is soft. Store, covered in refrigerator for up to one week.

INGREDIENTS

6	cantaloupe wedges, about half a melon
6	honeydew wedges, about half a melon
12	pieces thinly sliced prosciutto

Vinaigrette:

½	cup toasted Maui onion mustard
¼	cup rice vinegar
1	clove garlic, roasted
½	cup canola oil
	Salt and pepper to taste
	Fresh mint, chopped, for garnish

✳

Maui Onion Salsa Party Dip

INGREDIENTS

1	lb. smoked cheddar cheese
2	cups heavy whipping cream
1	cup Maui onion salsa
1	Tbsp. chopped fresh cilantro
	Corn chips for dipping

✳

Serve this smoky cheese dip with crunchy corn chips; blue corn chips are especially good. For a heartier dip, add chopped fresh ripe tomatoes and a couple of diced grilled chicken breasts. **Serves 6**

Place the cheese and cream in the top of a double boiler and place over simmering water. As the cheese melts, stir to incorporate the cream. When the mixture is well blended, add the salsa and cilantro and stir to mix. Transfer to a fondue pot or a large warm bowl. Serve with chips.

Glazed Baby Back Ribs, Two Ways

There's nothing better than glazed baby back pork ribs, tender, falling off the bone and flavorful. To do this, the ribs are boiled, baked, then grilled to obtain a smoky flavor. Add flavor as they cook with one of two sauces: one is piquant and spicy, the other is fruity with a little kick. Choose your sauce and you're on your way to the best tasting ribs! **Serves 4**

INGREDIENTS

2	slabs pork baby back ribs, about 1¾ pounds each
4	qt. water
¼	cup coarse-grained salt
¼	cup liquid smoke
	Hawaiian Pepper Jelly Sauce or Guava Chili Sauce (recipes follow)

✳

Bring water to a boil in a large stockpot. Add the salt and liquid smoke. When the salt has dissolved, add the ribs and bring water back to a boil. Adjust the heat to medium and cook the ribs until fork tender, about 1 to 1¼ hours. When the ribs are cooked, remove from liquid, drain well and cool.

Preheat oven to 350°F. Cut the racks in half and place on a baking sheet. Baste with the sauce. Bake in the oven for 20 to 30 minutes or until golden brown. Remove the ribs from the oven and cool.

Heat a grill. When the grill is hot, sear the ribs, basting with more sauce. Cook for a few minutes on each side to obtain smoky flavor. When the ribs are heated through and nicely browned remove from the grill. Cut ribs into portions and serve.

Glazed Baby Back Ribs, Two Ways

Hawaiian Pepper Jelly Sauce

INGREDIENTS

1   cup Hawaiian pepper jelly

¼   cup honey

1   Tbsp. minced fresh ginger

    Salt and pepper to taste

❋

In a blender, place the jelly, honey and ginger and blend at high speed until smooth, about 30 seconds. Season to taste with salt and pepper.

Guava Chili Sauce

INGREDIENTS

1   cup guava jam

1   cup sweet Thai chili sauce

❋

In a blender, place the jam and chili sauce and blend at high speed until smooth, about 30 seconds.

Pineapple Roasted Garlic and Mint Lobster Sticks

The ingredient list may look unusual but the combination of lobster and fruit works very well together. Cold-water Maine lobsters are well suited to this dish. **Serves 4**

INGREDIENTS

2   8 oz. lobster tails, uncooked

12   6-inch bamboo skewers

    Salt and pepper to taste

Sauce:

½   cup pineapple syrup

¼   cup unsalted butter

    cloves roasted garlic, minced (see page 9)

1   Tbsp. chopped fresh mint

Garnishes:

4½ - inch slices fresh pineapple

    Toasted black sesame seeds

    Toasted white sesame seeds

    Green onions, chopped

❋

Preheat oven to 350°F.

Remove the lobster meat from their shells and cut in half lengthwise. Cut each half of the tail into 3 strips on a diagonal. Thread each strip onto a skewer. Season with salt and pepper.

In a small saucepan heat the syrup, butter and garlic over medium heat; simmer 5 minutes. Add the mint and remove from heat.

Arrange the lobster skewers on a baking pan and brush with half of the sauce. Bake the lobster in the oven, until cooked but translucent, about 6 to 8 minutes.

Place the pineapple slices in the center of four plates. Stick the pointed end of 3 skewers into each pineapple slice on a slight angle. Drizzle the remaining sauce over each plate and garnish with sesame seeds and green onions. Serve.

Lobster Stuffed Yukon Gold Potato with Papaya Seed Dressing

Lobster is such a treat, its delicate, sweet meat so succulent and tasty. You could use crab or shrimp in place of the lobster in this recipe but lobster should be your first choice. **Serves 6**

Preheat oven to 350°F.

Using a small spoon hollow out the potato, being careful not to break the skin. Chop the potato flesh and place into a mixing bowl. Add the lobster meat to the potato.

In a small skillet, melt the butter over medium high heat and sauté the onion and mushrooms until onions are cooked and light brown. Transfer to the lobster potato mixture. Add the dressing and mix well. Fill the potato skins with the potato mixture and top with a slice of Swiss cheese. Bake for 10 to 15 minutes until the mixture is heated through and the cheese is melted.

Place the potato in a small soup bowl. Drizzle with crème fraiche; garnish with the caviar, green onions and parsley. Serve immediately.

INGREDIENTS

3	large Yukon gold potatoes, baked and cut in half
1	2-lb. fresh lobster, steamed, cooled, shelled and chopped
¼	cup unsalted butter
1	small Maui onion or other sweet onion, finely diced
6	crimini or button mushrooms, finely diced
½	cup papaya seed dressing
6	slices Swiss cheese

Garnishes:

Crème fraiche or sour cream

Orange tobiko caviar (flying fish roe)

Green onions, chopped

Fresh parsley, chopped

Shrimp Lumpia with Pohā Chili Dipping Sauce

Lumpia is a Filipino spring roll, crunchy on the outside and filled with goodies inside. This contemporary Pacific Rim-style version is a wonderful cocktail party hors d'oeurve. **Serves 4**

For the dipping sauce, place the jam, chili sauce, honey, and vinegar in a blender and blend until smooth. Slowly add the oil and blend until well mixed. Season to taste with salt and pepper. Set aside until ready to serve.

Butterfly each prawn by cutting in half lengthwise along the underside, leaving the topside attached. Open and flatten the prawn.

In a mixing bowl, mix the crab meat, onion, bell pepper, panko, five-spice and 1 egg.

Beat the remaining egg in a small bowl. Lay out one piece of the lumpia wrapper with the center point of the triangle to your right. Brush the edges with the egg. Place one prawn on the wrapper with the tail at the center point. Place 1 tablespoon of stuffing on each prawn. Fold the wrapper over the prawn, starting at the bottom point, fold left side edge over and continue to fold the wrapper to encase the prawn, leaving the tail exposed.

In a deep fryer or saucepan, heat oil. When the oil is hot (350°F), fry the lumpia, a couple at a time, about 3 to 4 minutes each or until golden brown. Remove from the oil and drain on paper towels.

Divide the lumpia among four plates and accompany with sauce. Garnish with sesame seeds and pickled ginger.

INGREDIENTS

Dipping sauce:

½ cup poha berry jam

¼ cup sweet Thai chili sauce

¼ cup macadamia nut blossom honey
      or other honey

½ cup rice vinegar

½ cup canola oil

    Salt and pepper to taste

Lumpia:

16 black tiger prawns (16-20 ct.), peeled
      with tail attached and deveined

8 oz. Alaskan snow crab meat

¼ Maui onion or other sweet onion,
      finely diced

¼ red bell pepper, finely diced

¼ cup panko flakes

½ tsp. Chinese five-spice

2 eggs

8 lumpia wrappers cut in half into triangles
      Oil for deep-frying

Garnishes:

    Sesame seeds

    Pickled ginger

Seared Foie Gras with Mango Chutney

Foie gras, duck liver, is appreciated by aficionados for its silky texture and distinctive flavor. Indulge a little in this wonderfully rich food. **Serves 4**

Heat a large frying pan over high heat. When the pan is hot, add the foie gras pieces and quickly sear on both sides until golden brown, about 30 to 45 seconds on each side. Remove from the pan and drain on a paper towel to absorb excess grease.

Drain the fat from the pan, leaving a teaspoon of the fat. Adjust heat to medium high and add the onion and garlic. Cook until lightly brown. Add the red wine to deglaze the pan, scraping any bits in the pan. Continue to cook, reducing the wine to about half. Add the mango chutney and pepper and mix well. Season to taste with salt if needed. Stir the butter into the mixture and remove from the heat as soon as the butter is melted.

To serve, divide the foie gras among four plates. Spoon the sauce over and around the foie gras. Garnish with mango fan and mint; serve immediately.

INGREDIENTS

4	3 oz. pieces foie gras, deveined and cleaned
½	small Maui onion, finely diced
1	tsp. garlic, minced
¼	cup Merlot or other red wine
1	cup mango chutney
1	tsp. fresh coarsely ground black pepper
	Salt to taste
2	tsp. unsalted butter, room temperature

Garnishes:

    Fresh ripe mango, sliced into fans

    Mint leaves, chopped

❋

Ham and Cheese on Rye, Maui-Style

Ham and Cheese on Rye, Maui-Style

This classic grilled ham and cheese sandwich on fresh rye bread is a tasty sensation with the addition of toasted Maui onion mustard. Sweet potato or breadfruit chips alongside make this a special island treat. Be sure to serve some extra mustard alongside for dipping. **Serves 2**

Preheat oven to 350°F.

On a sandwich board, lay out 2 slices of bread. Divide the ham, tomato and cheese evenly onto bread. Spread the mustard onto the remaining slices of bread and place on top of cheese to form sandwich.

Melt butter in a large skillet over medium high heat. Place sandwiches in pan and brown both sides. Transfer the pan to the oven and bake until sandwiches are golden brown and heated through, about 5 minutes.

Cut each sandwich into four triangles and arrange on two plates. Serve immediately.

INGREDIENTS

4	slices hearty rye bread
8	oz. thinly sliced smoked honey cured ham
4	slices vine ripened tomato
4	slices Swiss cheese
2	Tbsp. toasted Maui onion mustard
4	Tbsp. unsalted butter

"Monte Cristo" Sandwich, Hawaiian-Style

INGREDIENTS

2	slices Portuguese sweet bread
4	Tbsp. guava strawberry jam
2	oz. thinly sliced turkey breast
2	oz. thinly sliced smoked ham
2	slices Swiss cheese
2	eggs
¼	cup milk
1	tsp. cinnamon
2	Tbsp. unsalted butter
	Confectioners' sugar for dusting

❋

Portuguese sweet bread – an egg and butter-rich staple of the islands – and guava strawberry jam, add a unique twist to this classic lunchtime favorite. If sweet bread is not available, good quality sandwich bread will do.

Makes one sandwich

Place the bread on a sandwich board and spread each slice with jam. Layer the turkey, ham and cheese on one slice and top with the second slice to form sandwich.

In a flat bowl, whisk together the eggs, milk and cinnamon until well blended. Dip sandwich into the egg mixture, coating well.

Heat a small skillet over medium heat and add the butter. When the butter is melted, place the sandwich in the pan and cook until the egg has set and the bread is nicely browned. Turn and repeat on other side. Remove from the pan and place on a paper towel to drain and cool slightly.

Cut the sandwich diagonally, creating four triangles. Arrange on a warm plate with points facing up. Dust with sugar and serve with additional guava strawberry jam.

Maui Onion Salsa Steak Sandwich

INGREDIENTS

2	4-oz. center cut beef tenderloin steaks (filet mignon)
1	French bread or hoagie roll
2	Tbsp. unsalted butter, softened
½	tsp. minced garlic
3	slices vine ripened tomato
¼	cup Maui onion salsa
¼	cup roasted red bell pepper
¼	cup grated mozzarella cheese
	Salt and pepper to taste

❋

A great steak sandwich consists of quality meat like filet mignon, crusty French bread or hoagie roll and a tasty Maui onion salsa to add some spice. Here's how to do it. **Makes one sandwich**

Preheat a broiler or toaster oven.

Cut French bread or hoagie roll in half. Mix together butter and garlic and spread on cut halves. Place on a baking sheet and toast under a broiler until golden brown.

Heat a grill. When the grill is hot, grill steaks to desired doneness (120°F to 130°F for rare, 130°F to 135°F for medium rare, 140°F to 150°F for medium). Remove the steaks from grill and let rest for 5 to 10 minutes. (Alternatively, you can broil the steaks under the broiler.)

Place the steaks on the roll, top with tomatoes, salsa, pepper and cheese. Place under the broiler to melt the cheese. Cut in half to serve with additional salsa alongside.

Orange Mango Chicken on Focaccia

Marinating chicken breasts in Italian dressing tenderizes and helps to keep it moist. In this recipe, a little chili powder and citrus adds more spice and focaccia adds its chewiness, all adding up to a fresh approach to a chicken sandwich. **Serves 2**

In a small bowl, marinate the chicken with the dressing. Cover and refrigerate for at least 4 hours or overnight.

To cook, heat a grill or oven to 350°F. Remove the chicken from the marinade and sprinkle each piece with chili powder. Grill over hot coals or place on a baking sheet and into oven. Cook for 8 to 10 minutes or until done (160°F on a thermometer). Remove from oven.

Mix the butter and garlic together. Split the focaccia into four slices and spread the garlic butter over all sides. Place on a baking sheet and toast until lightly browned. Remove from the oven and place the chicken on the bottom portion of the focaccia. Spread the marmalade over the chicken. Cover with the cheese and place in the oven to melt cheese.

Remove from the oven and top with the tomato and lettuce. Place other halves of focaccia on top. Cut sandwich in half, diagonally and serve at once.

INGREDIENTS

2	pieces chicken breast, boneless and skinless, about 3 to 4 oz. each
¼	cup bottled Italian dressing
1	tsp. ancho chili powder or other chili powder
2	Tbsp. butter at room temperature
½	tsp. minced garlic
2	4-inch squares fresh focaccia
2	Tbsp. orange mango marmalade
2	slices Monterey Jack cheese
4	slices ripe tomato
2	leaves romaine lettuce

Maui Onion Salsa Chicken Burritos

Burritos are always popular, especially when there are lots of interesting textures and flavors inside. Don't forget the sour cream, guacamole and Maui onion salsa alongside to add even more flavor punch. **Serves 2**

INGREDIENTS

2	*pieces chicken breast, boneless and skinless, about 3 to 4 oz. each*
1	*cup Maui onion salsa*
2	*sun-dried tomato flour tortillas or any flour tortillas*
1	*cup steamed white rice*
1	*cup grated cheddar cheese*
½	*cup refried beans*

Garnishes:

Sour cream

Guacamole

Maui onion salsa

In a small bowl, marinate the chicken in ½ cup of the salsa. Cover and refrigerate for 3 to 4 hours or overnight.

To cook the chicken, heat a grill. When the grill is hot, drain the chicken, discarding the marinade. Grill the chicken for 3 to 4 minutes on each side or until cooked through (160°F on a thermometer). Remove from the grill, cool and cut into ½-inch dice.

Preheat oven to 400°F.

Lay out the tortillas and divide the beans, placing them in the center of each tortilla. Top the beans with the rice, chicken, remaining salsa and cheese. Roll each tortilla over the filling, tuck in the outer edges and roll to close. Place on a baking sheet and bake until lightly browned and cheese is melted, about 6 to 8 minutes. Cut in half and place on a warm plate to serve. Garnish with sour cream, guacamole and more salsa.

Passion Chili Chicken Quesadilla

The flavors of Latin America, Hawai'i and Asia come together in this perfect appetizer for a party or a wonderful light lunch with a tossed salad. I like to use large (12-inch) sun-dried tomato tortillas because they add another flavor dimension and lots of color. If you can't find any, plain flour tortillas will be fine. **Serves 2**

In a small bowl, marinate the chicken with the Italian dressing. Cover and refrigerate for at least 2 hours or overnight.

To cook the chicken, heat a grill or oven to 350°F. Remove the chicken from the marinade, draining the excess and discarding the marinade. Sprinkle each piece with cumin. Grill over hot coals or place on a baking sheet and roast in oven. Cook for 8 to 10 minutes or until cooked through (160°F on a thermometer). Remove from the grill or oven and cool. When the chicken is cool enough to handle, cut into ½-inch dice.

Increase oven temperature to 400°F.

Heat a small skillet over medium heat and add the oil. Add the onions and cook until onions are translucent and soft. Transfer onions to a small bowl. Add the jelly, chili paste and vinegar and mix well. Add the diced chicken and toss together.

Place the tortillas on a greased baking sheet. Spread chicken over half of each tortilla. Sprinkle with cheese. Fold the tortillas in half and place in the oven. Bake until golden brown and cheese has melted. Remove from the oven and cut each quesadilla into 4 wedges. Serve with greens, sour cream, guacamole and salsa. Garnish with green onions.

INGREDIENTS

2	pieces chicken breasts, boneless and skinless, about 3 to 4 oz. each
¼	cup bottled Italian dressing
1	tsp. ground cumin
1	tsp. canola oil
½	Maui onion or other sweet onion, diced
½	cup passion fruit jelly
½	tsp. sambal oelek or other chili garlic paste
1	tsp. rice vinegar
2	12-inch sun-dried tomato tortillas
1	cup shredded smoked cheddar cheese
	Salt and pepper to taste

Garnishes:

Baby greens or your favorite salad mix

Sour cream

Guacamole

Maui onion salsa

Green onions, chopped

Fresh Fish Quesadilla with Maui Onion Salsa

Fresh fish is the key to this tasty snack or party munchy. Mahi mahi or ono are good choice but any firm, white-fleshed fish will be just as delicious. If you can find flavored flour tortillas such as those made with sun-dried tomatoes, by all means use them. Otherwise, plain flour tortillas will do. **Serves 2**

INGREDIENTS

6	oz. fresh mahi mahi or ono filet, boneless and skinless
	Salt and pepper to taste
¼	cup canola oil
2	sun-dried tomato flour tortillas
½	cup shredded cheddar cheese
½	cup shredded Monterey Jack cheese
½	cup diced vine ripened tomato
½	cup Maui onion salsa

Garnishes:

Avocado, diced

Sour cream

Lime wedges

Maui onion salsa

✳

Heat a grill and when it is hot, season the fish with salt and pepper. Brush the fish with a little of the canola oil and grill until cooked through, about 6 to 8 minutes. Remove the fish from the grill. Flake fish with a fork or chop into small chunks.

Place tortillas on a flat surface. Divide fish onto half of each tortilla. Top with cheeses, tomato and salsa. Fold each tortilla in half.

Heat a large skillet or griddle over medium heat. Add the oil and when it is hot, place the filled tortillas in the pan. Brown each side and cook until ingredients are warm and cheeses are melted. Remove the quesadilla from the pan and place on a cutting board. Cut each quesadilla into four triangles and arrange on a heated plate. Serve with avocado, sour cream, lime wedges and more Maui onion salsa.

Fresh Fish Quesadilla with Maui Onion Salsa

Pineapple and Liliko'i Chicken Salad

Salads and Light Entrees

Candied Guava Macadamia Nut Salad

This unusual pairing of tropical fruits and nuts makes for a light and refreshing meal on a hot summer night. Red grape tomatoes, a sweet new variety, would be ideal in this salad. **Serves 4**

Preheat oven to 250°F.

For the guava coated macadamia nuts, place the guava jam and ginger in a blender and blend at high speed until smooth, about 10 seconds. Transfer to a small bowl and add the macadamia nuts, coating well. Spread the nuts on a greased baking sheet and bake in oven until golden brown, about 15 to 20 minutes. Remove from the oven, cool and break into bite-sized pieces.

To prepare vinaigrette, place the guava jam, ginger and vinegar in a blender and blend at high speed until smooth, about 30 seconds. Slowly add the oil and blend until well mixed. Season to taste with salt and pepper.

Divide the greens among four chilled salad plates. Arrange tomatoes around the greens. Drizzle vinaigrette over greens and tomato. Sprinkle the plate with the nuts and top with the carrots. Serve immediately.

INGREDIENTS

Guava Coated Macadamia Nuts:

½	cup guava jam
1	tsp. minced ginger
1	cup diced macadamia nuts

Vinaigrette:

½	cup guava jam
1	tsp. minced ginger
¼	cup rice vinegar
½	cup canola oil
	Salt and pepper to taste

Salad:

8	oz. baby salad greens or favorite salad mix
8	small tomatoes cut in half, such as cherry or red grape
¼	cup carrots, cut into fine strings or julienne

❋

Baby Spinach Salad with Apple Wood Smoked Bacon and Papaya Seed Dressing

INGREDIENTS

4   strips apple wood smoked bacon, diced

1   small Maui onion or other sweet onion, thinly sliced

½   cup papaya seed dressing

16 oz. fresh baby spinach, rinsed and well drained

Garnishes:

4   quail eggs, boiled, peeled and cut in quarters or 2 eggs

1   carrot, cut into fine string or fine julienne

1   red bell pepper, seeded and julienned

    Honey roasted macadamia nuts, chopped

✳

A traditional spinach salad is enhanced with a papaya seed dressing adding a little sweetness to balance the smoky bacon tidbits. Quail eggs, if you can find them, add an amusing touch. **Serves 4**

In a small skillet over medium high heat, cook the bacon until crisp. Remove the bacon from the pan and drain. Place the bacon in a salad bowl and add the onion and dressing, tossing together. Add the spinach and toss well to coat the spinach.

Divide the spinach among four chilled salad plates. Garnish with the eggs, carrot, bell pepper and nuts. Serve immediately.

Baby Spinach Salad with Apple Wood Smoked Bacon and Papaya Seed Dressing

Sweet Onion Salad with Honey Oriental Vinaigrette

Maui onions are among the sweetest in the world, grown on the slopes of Haleakalā, the dormant volcano that dominates the Maui landscape. If you can't find them, substitute another sweet onion. **Serves 4**

INGREDIENTS

4   small Maui onions or other sweet
      onion, peeled

4   tsp. unsalted butter

     Salt and pepper to taste

Vinaigrette:

1   tsp. minced ginger

1   tsp. sesame oil

¼   cup cider vinegar

¼   cup macadamia nut blossom honey

½   cup canola oil

1   tsp. toasted white sesame seeds

8   oz. baby salad greens or favorite salad mix

Garnishes:

     *Fresh ginger, finely julienned, deep-fried
      to crisp*

     Red bell pepper, finely diced

     Macadamia nuts, chopped

Preheat oven to 400°F.

Cut onions into quarters without cutting all the way through. Place the onions in a greased baking dish. Place 1 teaspoon of butter in the center of each onion. Sprinkle with salt and pepper and bake until lightly brown, about 10 to 15 minutes. Remove from the oven and let cool.

To make the vinaigrette, place the ginger, sesame oil, vinegar and honey into a blender and blend at high speed until smooth, about 30 seconds. Slowly add the oil and blend until well mixed. Season to taste with salt and pepper and stir in the sesame seeds.

Divide the greens among four chilled salad plates. Place one onion in the center of each plate. Drizzle a quarter of the vinaigrette over each onion and greens. Garnish with ginger, red bell pepper and nuts. Serve immediately.

✳

Pineapple and Liliko'i Chicken Salad

Liliko'i is a yellow skinned fruit with a yellow-orange pulp and black seeds with a tart and intense flavor. Made into a jelly, liliko'i, also known as passion fruit, is simply delicious! **Serves 4**

In a blender, place the syrup, jelly, vinegar and onion and blend at high speed until smooth, about 30 seconds. Slowly add the oil and blend until well mixed. Season to taste with salt and pepper.

Place the chicken into a bowl and toss with ½ cup of the vinaigrette. Marinate, covered and refrigerated for 3 to 4 hours or overnight. Cover and refrigerate remaining vinaigrette.

To cook the chicken, preheat oven to 350°F. Combine the Cajun spice and ancho chili powder. Remove the chicken from the marinade and discard marinade. Sprinkle each piece with the spice mixture. Place on a baking pan and cook in the oven for 10 to 12 minutes or until done (160°F on a thermometer). Remove from oven and cool.

While chicken is cooking, heat the rum and butter in a wide skillet over high heat. Allow the mixture to boil to burn off the alcohol, about 3 minutes. Carefully place pineapple halves into the pan, coating all sides of the pineapple. Remove the pan from the heat, cover with foil and place in the oven for 10 minutes. Remove from oven, uncover and cool. When cool enough to handle, cut the pineapple into 2-inch strips on a diagonal.

Place romaine lettuce in a bowl and toss with ½ cup of the vinaigrette. Divide the romaine among four chilled salad plates. Slice the chicken into thin diagonal strips and arrange around the greens. Drizzle remaining vinaigrette around the chicken. Garnish with pineapple strips, red pepper and tomatoes and serve immediately.

To do a chiffonade cut: Stack rinsed and dried romaine lettuce leaves. Cut crosswise into very thin strips.

INGREDIENTS

Vinaigrette:

¼	cup pineapple syrup
¼	cup liliko'i jelly
¼	cup rice vinegar
½	Maui onion or other sweet onion, diced
¼	cup canola oil
	Salt and pepper to taste
4	pieces chicken breast, boneless and skinless, about 3 to 4 oz. each
2	Tbsp. Cajun spice
2	Tbsp. ancho chili powder or other chili powder

Salad:

4	Tbsp. dark rum
4	Tbsp. unsalted butter
1	fresh pineapple skinned, cored and cut in half lengthwise
1	head romaine lettuce, chiffonade cut
1	medium red bell pepper, cored, seeded and cut into fine julienne
8	small tomatoes: cherry, grape or teardrop

Chicken Papaya Salad

Fresh papaya from Hawai'i is lusciously sweet and flavorful, the perfect "cup" for a well-seasoned chicken salad with crunchy macadamia nuts. This is just right for lunch or a light supper. **Serves 4**

INGREDIENTS

4	pieces chicken breast, boneless and skinless, about 3 to 4 oz. each
½	cup bottled Italian dressing
1	Tbsp. Cajun spice seasoning
2	fresh ripe papayas
¼	cup chopped macadamia nuts
¼	cup grilled diced Maui onion or other sweet onion
½	cup papaya seed dressing
1	Tbsp. fresh coarsely ground black pepper
	Salt to taste

Garnishes:

Micro greens

Cherry tomatoes

Fresh parsley, chopped

※

In a bowl, marinate the chicken breasts with the dressing. Marinate, covered and refrigerated, for 3 to 4 hours or overnight.

To cook the chicken, preheat oven to 350°F. Remove the chicken from the refrigerator and drain the marinade, discarding marinade. Sprinkle each piece with the Cajun spice and place on a baking sheet. Bake the chicken in the oven for 8 to 10 minutes or until cooked (160°F on a thermometer). Remove the chicken from the oven and cool. When cool, cut the chicken into 1-inch dice and place in a bowl.

Cut the papayas in half, lengthwise. Carefully scoop out the seeds and discard.

To the chicken, add the nuts, onion, dressing, pepper and salt to taste. Toss together gently. Divide the chicken among the papaya halves and chill until ready to serve. Garnish with micro greens, tomatoes and parsley.

Roasted Squab Breast Salad with Hawaiian Chili Pepper Vinaigrette

There's nothing like perfectly cooked squab, its subtle characteristics enhanced by a well-seasoned vinaigrette. Serve this squab breast over a salad of wild field greens or your favorite salad mix – just make it crisp and fresh! **Serves 4**

In a large nonreactive bowl, place all the marinade ingredients. Add the squab and marinate, covered and refrigerated, for 4 to 6 hours.

To cook the squab, preheat oven to 375°F. Remove squab from refrigerator and drain the marinade, discarding. Place squab in a roasting pan and roast for 4 minutes or until medium rare. Remove squab from the oven and cool. Slice each breast into 2 or 3 pieces on the diagonal.

To make the vinaigrette, place the jelly, vinegar, onion, and basil in a blender and blend at high speed until smooth, about 30 seconds. Slowly add the oil and blend until well mixed. Taste and adjust seasoning with salt and pepper.

Divide the salad greens among four salad plates. Place squab on top, fanning the slices. Drizzle vinaigrette over the squab and greens. Garnish with carrots and serve.

INGREDIENTS

4   large squab breasts, skinless and boneless

Marinade:
1   medium Maui onion, or other sweet onion, sliced
1   tsp. minced garlic
1   stalk celery, chopped
1   large carrot, chopped
¼   cup balsamic vinegar
¼   cup extra virgin olive oil
1   tsp. chopped tarragon
1   Tbsp. chopped parsley
1   tsp. salt
1   Tbsp. fresh coarsely ground black pepper

Vinaigrette:
½   cup Hawaiian pepper jelly
¼   cup rice vinegar
¼   Maui onion or other sweet onion, diced
2   leaves fresh sweet basil
¼   cup canola oil
    Salt and pepper to taste
4   cups field greens or your favorite salad mix
    Carrots, cut into strings or fine julienne

Salad of Muscovy Duck Breast with Pineapple-Papaya Vinaigrette

INGREDIENTS

2 whole Muscovy duck breasts

Vinaigrette:

½ cup pineapple and papaya jam

¼ cup rice wine vinegar

½ small Maui onion or other sweet onion, diced

½ cup canola oil

Salt and freshly ground black pepper to taste

Salad and garnishes:

4 cups baby greens or your favorite salad mix

1 papaya, peeled and seeded, sliced into 8 wedges

1 cup finely diced fresh pineapple

8 cherry tomatoes, cut in half

1 cup pea sprouts or other sprouts

Serves 4

For the vinaigrette, place the jam, vinegar and onion in a blender and blend at high speed until smooth, about 30 seconds. Slowly add the oil and blend until well mixed. Season to taste with salt and pepper.

Cut the duck breasts in half, removing any cartilage. Place the duck pieces in a nonreactive bowl, add ½ cup of the vinaigrette and mix thoroughly. Marinate for at least 4 hours or overnight, covered, in the refrigerator.

To cook the duck, preheat oven to 450°F. Place the duck in a baking pan, skin side up. Roast the duck until skin is brown or for 6 to 8 minutes for medium doneness. Lower oven temperature to 350°F and continue to cook for a few more minutes if you want the duck to be well done. Remove the duck from the oven and cool while you prepare the salad.

Place the greens in a salad bowl and toss with ¼ cup of the vinaigrette. Divide among four chilled salad plates.

Slice each piece of duck into 4 pieces on the diagonal. Arrange the duck on the greens along with papaya, pineapple and tomatoes. Drizzle each plate with more vinaigrette. Garnish with sprouts and serve.

INGREDIENTS

16 baby carrots, washed and peeled

1 Tbsp. unsalted butter

1 tsp. minced ginger

¼ cup pineapple syrup

Salt and pepper to taste

Garnish:

Fresh parsley, chopped

Pineapple and Ginger Glazed Baby Carrots

Pineapple and a hint of ginger are truly a match made in heaven for carrots. You may want to double this recipe – it's that good! **Serves 4**

Prepare a bowl of ice water.

Bring a small saucepan of water to a boil. Add the carrots and cook for 4 to 5 minutes or until cooked but still firm. Drain the carrots and immerse in ice water to stop the cooking process. Drain again and set aside.

In a small sauté pan over high heat, melt the butter. Add the ginger and cook until lightly browned. Add the pineapple syrup, reduce heat and simmer for 1 minute. Add the carrots and coat with the sauce. Season to taste with salt and pepper. Transfer carrots to a serving dish and pour sauce over. Sprinkle with parsley and serve.

'Ahi Stuffed Tomato with Papaya Seed Dressing

Ahi is tuna – yellow fin or big eye – that is found in the deep waters of the Pacific Ocean. Prized in Hawai'i for sashimi (raw fish), 'ahi is often cut into small dice and seasoned, a dish called poke. Here's a Hawaiian-Italian version of this dish paired with good ripe tomatoes. **Serves 6**

Cut the tops off the tomatoes. Using a melon baller or spoon, scoop out the flesh of the tomatoes, being careful not to pierce the outer skin. Place tomatoes on a paper towel, cut side down, to drain.

Finely dice the tomato flesh and place in a large nonreactive mixing bowl. Add the 'ahi, capers, onion, cilantro, pepper and dressing and mix thoroughly. Season with salt to taste. Spoon the mixture into each hollowed tomato. Place on a plate, cover and refrigerate for 1 hour or until ready to serve.

To serve, decorate four plates with micro greens and place a tomato on each plate. Garnish with carrots and more papaya seed dressing.

INGREDIENTS

6	large vine ripened tomatoes
1	lb. fresh sashimi grade 'ahi, cut into ½-inch dice
1	Tbsp. capers, drained and chopped
1	Maui onion or other sweet onion, finely diced
1	Tbsp. chopped fresh cilantro
1	tsp. fresh coarsely ground black pepper
½	cup papaya seed dressing
	Coarse grain salt to taste

Garnishes:
Organic micro greens
Carrots, cut into strings or fine julienne

Diver Sea Scallop Salad with Pineapple Ginger Vinaigrette

INGREDIENTS

Vinaigrette:

¼   cup pineapple syrup

¼   cup rice vinegar

½   small Maui onion or other sweet
     onion, diced

1   Tbsp. chopped fresh mint

1   Tbsp. thinly sliced pickled ginger

½   cup canola oil

     Salt and pepper to taste

12   jumbo (U-10) sea scallops

1   Tbsp. extra virgin olive oil

Salad:

4   cups salad greens of choice

½   cup finely diced fresh pineapple

½   cup finely julienned green onions

¼   cup carrot strings or fine julienne

4   sprigs fresh mint

Diver sea scallops are handpicked and not treated with any chemicals so their quality and texture are excellent. Search them out for a real treat. Remember, cook scallops rare to medium to preserve their natural flavor and texture.

Serves 4

In a blender, place the syrup, vinegar, onion, mint and ginger and blend at high speed until smooth, about 30 seconds. Slowly add the oil and blend until well mixed. Season with salt and pepper to taste. Set aside.

In a small bowl, toss the sea scallops with the olive oil and salt and pepper. Heat a griddle or nonstick frying pan over high heat. When the pan is hot, sear the scallops until golden brown, turning to sear the other side. Cook until scallops are nicely browned and cooked to medium doneness, about 2 to 3 minutes. Remove scallops from pan.

In a large bowl, toss the salad greens with ½ cup of the vinaigrette. Divide the greens among four plates and arrange 3 scallops on each plate. Drizzle scallops with the remaining vinaigrette. Garnish with the pineapple, green onions, carrot and mint.

Diver Sea Scallop Salad with Pineapple Ginger Vinaigrette

Grilled Tiger Prawns with Pineapple and Papaya Salsa

Seafood and Fish

Grilled Tiger Prawns with Pineapple and Papaya Salsa

This is a quick and refreshing recipe to prepare on a hot summer afternoon. You will impress your friends with this unique blend of tropical fruits that will remind you of the taste of aloha. **Serves 4**

Place the jam, vinegar and onion into a blender and blend at high speed until smooth, about 30 seconds. Slowly add the oil and blend until well mixed. Season to taste with salt and pepper.

In a nonreactive mixing bowl, toss the prawns in ½ cup of the vinaigrette, cover and chill for 1 hour.

In another bowl toss together the pineapple, papaya, kiwi, strawberries, cilantro, sambal, honey and 2 tablespoons of the vinaigrette. Cover and chill.

To cook the prawns, heat a grill. When the grill is hot, remove the prawns from the marinade, drain and discard the marinade. Grill the prawns, turning, until cooked, about 3 to 4 minutes.

Divide the fruit salsa among four plates and arrange the prawns around the salsa. Drizzle with the remaining vinaigrette and garnish with sesame seeds and micro greens.

INGREDIENTS

12 jumbo tiger prawns (11-15 ct.), peeled and deveined

Vinaigrette:
½ cup pineapple and papaya jam
¼ cup rice vinegar
½ small Maui onion or other sweet onion, diced
½ cup canola oil
Salt and pepper to taste

Salsa:
½ cup fresh pineapple, finely diced
½ cup fresh papaya, finely diced
¼ cup kiwi, finely diced
¼ cup strawberries, finely diced
1 tsp. fresh cilantro, chopped
1 tsp. sambal oelek or other chili garlic paste
1 tsp. macadamia nut blossom honey or other honey

Garnishes:
Toasted black sesame seeds
Toasted white sesame seeds
Micro greens or other sprouts

16 tiger prawns (16-20 ct.), peeled
    and deveined

1   Tbsp. canola oil

1   tsp. fresh ginger, minced

1   Maui onion or other sweet onion,
    thinly sliced

½   cup Hawaiian pepper jelly

4   heads baby bok choy

½   cup julienned carrot

1   Tbsp. fresh cilantro, chopped

    Salt and pepper to taste

Garnishes:

    Toasted white sesame seeds

    Green onions, chopped

※

1   lb. small fresh clams, rinsed and drained

1   Tbsp. sesame oil

1   tsp. minced ginger

¼   cup orange mango marmalade

1   tsp. Thai red curry paste

1   tsp. fermented black beans, rinsed
    and chopped

¼   cup sake

1   tsp. chopped cilantro

¼   cup unsalted butter

Garnishes:

    Tomato, finely diced

    Green onions, finely chopped

    Roasted sesame seeds

Hawaiian Chili Pepper Glazed Tiger Prawns

Hawaiian chili peppers are small but fiery and when it's made into a jelly, the sweet-hot combination is terrific. Serve this dish with steamed white rice. **Serves 4**

Heat the oil in a wok or large skillet over high heat. Add the ginger and Maui onion and lightly brown, about 1 minute. Add the jelly, bok choy, carrot and prawns and cook together, tossing and stirring. Cook for 3 to 4 minutes or until vegetables are wilted but still crunchy and prawns are cooked through. Add the cilantro and toss together. Remove from the heat and divide among four plates. Garnish with sesame seeds and green onions.

Orange Mango Black Bean Clams

Fermented black beans are a terrific seasoning, adding the salt component to a sauce. Orange mango marmalade balances the powerful flavor of black beans and the heat of the chili in the curry paste just perfectly. **Serves 2**

Heat the oil in a wok or large skillet over high heat. Add the ginger and lightly brown. Add the marmalade, curry paste and black beans. Reduce the heat and simmer, stirring, for about 2 minutes. Add the clams, sake, cilantro and butter and stir well. Cover and cook for 2 to 3 minutes or until all the clams have opened. Remove from the heat and scoop clams and sauce into a bowl. Garnish with tomatoes, green onions and sesame seeds and serve immediately.

Orange Mango Black Bean Clams

Orange Mango Lobster and Almond Stir-fry

INGREDIENTS

1½ lb.	fresh lobster, cooked and shelled
1	Tbsp. sesame oil
1	tsp. ginger, minced
½	Maui onion or other sweet onion, sliced thin
¼	cup orange mango marmalade
½	tsp. sambal oelek or other chili garlic paste
¼	cup sake
½	cup fresh ripe mango, preferably Hayden, cut into ½-inch dice
½	cup Ka'ū orange segments, or other sweet orange, peeled and chopped
¼	cup almonds, roasted and sliced
	Salt and pepper to taste

Garnishes:

Green onions, chopped

Toasted white sesame seeds

Carrot strings or fine julienne

※

Ka'ū is located on the southern portion of the island of Hawai'i and it is the home of Ka'ū oranges. These are very special oranges: not very pretty on the outside but juicy, very sweet and flavorful on the inside. In this dish with mango and lobster, it's incredible! **Serves 4**

Cut lobster into bite-sized pieces.

Heat the oil in a wok or large skillet over high heat. Add the ginger and onion and cook until lightly brown, tossing with a spatula. Add the marmalade, sambal and sake and reduce heat to a simmer. Cook for 1 minute to blend the flavors.

Add the lobster, mango, orange and almonds and toss together until heated through. Season to taste with salt and pepper. Remove from the heat. Divide mixture among four warmed dinner plates. Garnish with green onions, sesame seeds and carrots and serve immediately.

Orange Mango Lobster and Almond Stir-fry

Passion Fruit Ginger Jumbo Shrimp Stir-fry

Stir-frying is a popular cooking technique in Hawai'i because everything is kept crunchy and cooked just right. That's particularly important with shrimp so be sure to add it towards the end of the cooking time. The fruity marinade helps to keep everything moist and flavorful. **Serves 4**

INGREDIENTS

12	jumbo (11-15 ct.) Mexican white shrimp
2	Tbsp. sesame oil
1	tsp. minced fresh ginger
1	Maui onion or other sweet onion, sliced thin
1	carrot, thinly sliced on a diagonal
4	baby bok choy or other green leafy cabbage
4	crimini or button mushrooms, sliced
¾	cup passion fruit jelly
	Salt and pepper to taste

Garnishes:
Toasted white sesame seeds
Green onions, chopped

✳

In a wok or large frying pan, heat the sesame oil over high heat. Toss in the ginger and stir-fry for 30 seconds. Add the onion, carrot, bok choy and mushrooms and cook, stirring and tossing several times.

When the vegetables are half cooked, about 1 to 2 minutes, add the shrimp and passion fruit jelly and cook, stirring and tossing. When the shrimp are cooked, about 2 to 3 minutes, season with salt and pepper and remove from the heat. Serve family style or on individual plates, garnished with roasted sesame seeds and chopped green onions.

INGREDIENTS

1	lb. bay scallops
1	cup unsalted butter, at room temperature
½	cup guava jam
2	Tbsp. sambal oelek or other chili garlic sauce
½	Maui onion or other sweet onion, diced
1	tsp. minced fresh ginger
	Salt and pepper to taste

Garnishes:
Fresh cilantro, chopped
Toasted black sesame seeds

✳

Guava Chili Glazed Bay Scallops

This is a very simple recipe with a very complex flavor profile that blends Hawaiian and Asian flare. Bay scallops, sweet and succulent, make this dish outstanding. Jasmine rice would be an ideal accompaniment. **Serves 4**

Preheat oven to 400°F.

In a food processor, place the butter, jam, sambal, onion and ginger and process until smooth. Season with salt and pepper to taste.

Divide the scallops among four individual ovenproof casserole dishes. Divide the butter mixture over the scallops. Bake for 5 to 7 minutes or until scallops are cooked and lightly browned. Remove from oven, garnish with cilantro and sesame seeds and serve.

Island Spiced Ono with Guava Strawberry Fruit Salsa

Ono, a relative of the king mackerel, is a very meaty, steak-like fish that is plentiful during the summer months in Hawai'i. It is wonderful on the grill as well as sautéed; be careful not to overcook this fish as it tends to dry out quickly. **Serves 2**

Place strawberries, pineapple, kiwi, mango, and jam in a small mixing bowl. Toss and mix and refrigerate until ready to serve.

Mix the Cajun seasoning and five-spice in a shallow dish. Lightly dust each filet with the seasoning mix, covering both sides. Heat a skillet over medium heat and add the oil. When the oil is hot, add the fillets and cook until firm, about 8 minutes per inch of thickness, and brown on both sides. Remove the fish from the heat and place on paper towel to absorb excess grease.

Place each filet in the center of a warm dinner plate. Using a slotted spoon divide fruit salsa among the plates. Garnish with cilantro and serve immediately.

INGREDIENTS

Fruit salsa:

2	*strawberries, finely diced*
¼	*cup finely diced fresh pineapple*
1	*kiwi, peeled and diced*
¼	*cup diced fresh mango*
½	*cup guava strawberry jam*
2	*6 oz. ono steaks*
4	*Tbsp. Cajun seafood seasoning*
	Pinch of Chinese five-spice
4	*Tbsp. canola oil*
	Fresh cilantro sprigs

Sautéed Opakapaka with Guava Strawberry Beurre Blanc

Opakapaka is the Hawaiian pink snapper, perhaps the most prized fish in the islands. It is light and delicate, moist and flaky but with a nice firmness to the flesh. Sautéing is the best way to prepare this fish and a tropical beurre blanc makes it the best ever. **Serves 2**

INGREDIENTS

6	oz. opakapaka filets, boneless and skinless
¼	cup all-purpose flour
¼	cup canola oil
1	tsp. minced Maui onion or other sweet onion
¼	cup chardonnay or other white wine
¼	cup heavy whipping cream
2	Tbsp. guava strawberry jam
¼	cup unsalted butter
	Salt and pepper to taste

Garnishes:
Strawberries, sliced into fans
Fresh parsley, chopped

✳

Lightly dust the filets in flour. Heat a skillet over medium high heat and add the oil. When the oil is hot, place the fish filets in the pan and lightly brown on both sides. Add the onion and wine and continue to cook as the wine reduces. When the fish is cooked (allow 8 minutes per inch of thickness), remove from the pan and keep warm.

Add the cream and jam to the pan and whisk to blend. Cook over medium heat until liquid is reduced and sauce is slightly thickened. Adjust the heat to low and whisk in the butter, incorporating well. Season to taste with salt and pepper.

Place each filet in the center of two warmed dinner plates. Ladle sauce over the filets and garnish with strawberry fan and chopped parsley. Serve immediately.

Sautéed Opakapaka with Guava Strawberry Beurre Blanc

Guava Almond Crusted Mahi Mahi

Fish – especially fresh mahi mahi from Hawaiian waters – and almonds are a perfect combination, especially when there's a Hawaiian twist. **Serves 4**

INGREDIENTS

4	6 oz. mahi mahi filets, boneless and skinless
1	cup guava syrup
1	tsp. minced fresh ginger
1	cup blanched sliced almonds
¼	cup unsalted butter
	Salt and pepper to taste

Preheat oven to 400°F.

Heat the syrup slowly in a small saucepan over medium heat. Add the ginger, almonds and butter, stirring and blending. When the butter has melted and is well incorporated, remove from the heat and cool to room temperature.

Place the fish in a greased baking dish. Using a slotted spoon, scoop the almond mixture and coat the top of each fish filet. Reserve the remaining guava sauce.

Bake the fish until golden brown and cooked through, about 8 minutes per inch of thickness. Meanwhile, reheat the remaining guava sauce in a small saucepan.

Place each fish filet in the center of a warm dinner plate. Drizzle guava sauce over the fish and serve.

Poached Salmon with Toasted Maui Onion Mustard Beurre Blanc

S almon is an oily, full flavored fish that pairs well with a butter sauce with a mustardy twist.

Serves 4

To prepare the poaching liquid for the salmon, place the fish stock, onion, carrot, celery, bay leaves and peppercorns in a wide saucepan and bring to a boil over high heat. Reduce the heat to medium-low and simmer for 15 minutes.

Using a slotted spoon or spatula, place the salmon filets into the hot liquid and cook about 6 to 8 minutes or until cooked through. Remove the fish from the liquid, place on a platter and keep warm.

To make the beurre blanc, heat a saucepan over medium heat and add the oil. When the oil is hot, add the shallots and sauté until lightly brown. Add the wine and vermouth and bring to a boil. Adjust the heat to medium low and reduce the liquid by half. Add the mustard and cream and simmer for 3 minutes. Whisk in the butter and when it has been well incorporated into the sauce, remove the sauce from the heat.

Ladle about ¼ cup of the sauce onto a heated dinner plate. Place the salmon filet in the center of the sauce. Garnish with tarragon and flowers and serve immediately.

INGREDIENTS

4   6 oz. salmon filets, boneless and skinless

Poaching liquid:

4   cups fish stock or clam juice

1   small Maui onion or other sweet onion, thinly sliced

1   carrot, chopped

1   stalk celery, chopped

2   bay leaves

1   Tbsp. whole black peppercorns

Beurre blanc:

1   tsp. minced fresh shallots

1   Tbsp. canola oil

¼   cup dry white wine

¼   cup vermouth

½   cup toasted Maui onion mustard

½   cup heavy whipping cream

½   cup unsalted butter

   Salt and pepper to taste

Garnishes:

   Fresh tarragon, chopped

   Fresh edible flowers

✳

Guava Barbecued Nairagi

Nairagi is striped marlin, considered the best eating of the marlin species. Its light pink flesh is firm with a pleasant flavor that is well liked in the islands. A smoky, spicy and slightly sweet treatment of this fish is wonderful. **Serves 4**

INGREDIENTS

4	6 oz. center cut nairagi steaks, boneless
1	cup guava grilling sauce
1	Tbsp. minced pickled ginger
1	tsp. wasabi paste
	Salt and pepper to taste

Garnishes:

White sesame seeds

Garlic chives or regular chives, chopped

Soy sauce mixed with wasabi paste

✳

In a small saucepan, heat the sauce with the ginger and wasabi over medium heat. Simmer for 5 minutes. Remove from the heat and cool.

Place the fish in nonreactive dish and pour the sauce over. Cover and refrigerate for 3 to 4 hours.

To cook the fish, heat a grill. When the grill is hot, remove the fish from the sauce and cook the fish for 2 to 3 minutes per side. When the fish is cooked (allow 8 minutes per inch of thickness), remove from the grill. Place the filets on plates and sprinkle with chives and sesame seeds. Serve with soy-wasabi sauce on the side.

Guava Barbecued Nairagi

Mango Chutney and Sweet Bread Stuffed Cornish Game Hens

Meat and Poultry

Guava Barbecued New York Steak

If you can get prime beef, by all means use it. Otherwise look for choice Black Angus beef. Plan ahead: it's important to marinate the beef for at least 12 hours or overnight. **Serves 4**

In a small saucepan, heat the sauce with the garlic, simmering for about 5 minutes. Remove from heat and cool.

In a nonreactive bowl, place the steaks and ¾ cup of the marinade. Marinate, covered and refrigerated, for at least 12 hours or overnight. Cover and refrigerate remaining marinade.

To cook the steaks, heat a grill. When the grill is hot, remove the steaks from the marinade, discarding the marinade. Grill the steaks to desired doneness (120°F to 130°F for rare, 130°F to 135°F for medium rare, 140°F to 150°F for medium). Remove the steaks from the grill and let the steak rest for 5 to 10 minutes.

Heat the remaining marinade in a small saucepan. Cut each steak into strips on a diagonal and arrange on a warm platter. Drizzle with the remaining marinade, garnish with Fried Maui Onion Rings and serve.

INGREDIENTS

4	12 oz. New York strip loin steaks
1	cup guava grilling sauce
1	tsp. minced garlic
	Salt and pepper to taste

Garnish:
Fried Maui Onion Rings (recipe follows)

※

Fried Maui Onion Rings

INGREDIENTS

1	Maui onion or other sweet onion, thinly sliced into rings
½	cup all-purpose flour
	Salt and pepper to taste
	Oil for deep-frying

✳

In a shallow bowl, mix the flour, salt and pepper. Toss the onion in the seasoned flour and shake off the excess.

Heat oil in a deep fryer or saucepan to 375°F. When the oil is hot, fry the onion rings until golden brown. Remove the onion rings from the oil and place on a paper towel to drain. Season again with salt and pepper and set aside.

Pohā Glazed Pork Chops

The secret to these tender and succulent pork chops is a two-step cooking process and a mouthwatering marinade. For smoky flavor use kiawe (mesquite) wood on the grill. **Serves 4**

INGREDIENTS

4	8 oz. pork chops
	Marinade:
½	cup pohā berry jam
¼	cup sweet Thai chili sauce
¼	cup honey
½	cup rice vinegar
½	cup canola oil
	Salt and pepper to taste
½	cup water

✳

In a blender, place the jam, chili sauce, honey and vinegar and blend at high speed until smooth, about 30 seconds. Slowly add the oil and blend until well mixed. Season to taste with salt and pepper.

Place the pork chops in a flat dish in a single layer. Pour half the marinade over the pork chops, coating well. Cover and refrigerate for at least 8 hours or overnight to help tenderize the meat. Cover and refrigerate remaining marinade.

To cook the pork chops, preheat oven to 350°F.

Heat a grill and when it is hot, remove the pork chops from the marinade, discarding the marinade. Sear and cook the pork chops, turning to brown both sides. Cook the pork chops to get smoky flavor but not all the way through. Remove the pork chops from the grill and place in a baking pan.

Pour ½ cup of water into the pan and cover with foil. Place the pork chops in the oven and bake for 8 to 10 minutes until they are almost cooked (just under 150°F on a thermometer). Remove foil and cook an additional 2 minutes to brown.

Remove the pork chops from the oven and let rest for 5 minutes before serving. Heat remaining marinade in a small saucepan. Drizzle the pork chops with the remaining marinade and serve.

Pohā Glazed Pork Chops

Guava Marinated Pork Chops on the Grill

The secret to cooking pork chops on the grill is a low fire to cook the chops slowly, maintaining their moisture and succulence. The exotic flavor of guava adds a distinctive touch to grilled pork chops. **Serves 4**

INGREDIENTS

4	*8 oz. center cut pork chops*

Marinade:

1	*cup guava grilling sauce*
1	*tsp. minced ginger*
1	*Tbsp. minced Maui onion or other sweet onion*
	Salt and pepper to taste

In a small saucepan over medium heat, combine the sauce, ginger and onion and heat for 5 minutes to blend the flavors. Remove from heat and cool.

Place the pork chops in a shallow dish and pour the sauce over. Marinate for 6 to 8 hours or overnight, covered, in refrigerator.

To cook the pork chops, heat a grill. When the coals are hot, allow them to cool to medium. Remove the pork chops from the marinade and drain well; discard marinade. Place pork chops over coals over medium low heat. Grill for 15 to 20 minutes or until cooked (150°F on a thermometer). Remove the pork chops from the grill and allow to rest for 5 minutes before serving.

Grilled Pork Chop with Toasted Maui Onion Mustard

M ustard is a good friend of pork and grilling adds that smoky flavor that's a winner every time. **Serves 4**

In a blender, place the mustard, vinegar and garlic and blend at high speed until smooth, about 30 seconds. Slowly add the oil, incorporating well. Season to taste with salt and pepper.

Place the pork chops in a nonreactive bowl. Pour half the marinade over the chops. Cover the bowl and refrigerate for 6 to 8 hours or overnight. Cover and refrigerate remaining marinade.

To cook the pork chops, heat a grill. When the grill is hot, allow it to cool to medium. Remove the pork chops from the marinade, drain and discard marinade. Place the chops on the grill. Cook for 12 to 15 minutes or until cooked (150°F on a thermometer). Remove from the grill and let stand for 5 minutes before serving.

Heat the remaining marinade in a small saucepan. Drizzle the remaining marinade over and around the chop. Garnish with Fried Maui Onion Rings and parsley.

INGREDIENTS

4   6 oz. center cut pork chops

Marinade:

1   cup toasted Maui onion mustard

¼   cup rice vinegar

1   clove garlic, roasted

½   cup canola oil

    Salt and pepper to taste

Garnishes:

    Fried Maui Onion Rings (see page 52)

    Fresh parsley, minced

Macadamia Nut Honey Glazed Pork Tenderloin

Pork tenderloin is that small, tender strip prized like beef tenderloin. Keep it moist and succulent by marinating and cooking it just right. A side dish of chilled applesauce is always a nice accompaniment to pork. **Serves 4**

INGREDIENTS

2   *whole pork tenderloins, about 10 to 12 oz. each*

Marinade:

½   *cup macadamia nut blossom honey*

½   *cup Dijon mustard*

¼   *cup cider vinegar*

¼   *cup canola oil*

1½ *tsp. fresh coarsely ground black pepper*

    Salt to taste

Garnishes:

    Crisp bacon bits

    Diced macadamia nuts

✳

In a blender, place the honey, mustard and vinegar and blend at high speed until smooth, about 30 seconds. Slowly add the oil and blend until well mixed. Add the pepper and season to taste with salt.

Place the tenderloins in a bowl and pour the marinade over the pork. Marinate, for 3 to 4 hours, covered and refrigerated, or overnight.

To cook the pork, preheat oven to 325°F.

Drain the pork from the marinade, discarding marinade. Place the pork in a roasting pan. Roast about 30 minutes or until cooked (150°F on a thermometer). Remove the pork from the oven and allow to rest 5 minutes.

To serve, slice the pork thin and fan one half of each tenderloin onto a warm plate. Spoon pan drippings over the pork. Garnish with bacon bits and macadamia nuts and serve.

Oven Roasted Rack of Lamb with Pineapple and Papaya

Rack of lamb is one of the easiest foods to prepare. Good quality lamb with a terrific marinade based on tropical fruits will make your lamb outstanding. **Serves 4**

Cut the lamb into 2-bone chops and remove meat from the end of the bones to expose the bones. Place the chops in a roasting pan.

In a blender, place the jam, vinegar, ginger and pepper and blend at high speed until smooth, about 30 seconds. Slowly add the oil and blend until well mixed. Pour half of the marinade over the lamb chops and marinate for 3 to 4 hours or overnight, covered and refrigerated. Cover and refrigerate remaining marinade.

To cook the lamb chops, preheat oven to 400°F.

Roast the lamb chops for 10 to 15 minutes or until desired temperature is reached (125°F for rare, 130°F for medium rare).

Heat the remaining marinade in a small saucepan over medium heat. Arrange the lamb chops on a large platter and drizzle with half of the remaining marinade. Garnish with Fried Maui Onion Rings and fresh chopped parsley. Serve remaining marinade alongside.

INGREDIENTS

2 racks of lamb, 8 bones each

Marinade:

⅛ cup pineapple and papaya jam

¼ cup rice vinegar

1 tsp. fresh ginger, minced

1 Tbsp. coarsely ground fresh black pepper

½ cup canola oil

Garnishes:

Fried Maui Onion Rings (see page 52)

Fresh parsley, chopped

Roasted Rack of Lamb with Hawaiian Pepper Jelly

Hawaiian chili peppers are tiny but fiery so this pepper jelly marinade will spice up a rack of lamb quite nicely. Pohā berry jam is a great accompaniment; steamed white rice and vegetables, too. **Serves 4**

INGREDIENTS

2   racks of lamb, 8 bones each

Marinade:

1   cup Hawaiian pepper jelly

¼   cup rice vinegar

1   Tbsp. roasted garlic, about 3 cloves
      (see page 9)

¼   cup chopped fresh sweet basil

½   cup canola oil

1   Tbsp. coarsely ground fresh black pepper

      Salt to taste

Garnish:

      Fried Maui Onion Rings (see page 52)

Cut the lamb into 2-bone chops and remove the meat from the end of the bones to expose the bones. Sprinkle with black pepper.

In a blender, place the jelly, vinegar, garlic and basil and blend at high speed until smooth, about 30 seconds. Slowly add the oil and blend until well mixed.

Place the lamb chops into a large mixing bowl and add the marinade, coating the chops well. Marinate for 3 to 4 hours or overnight, covered and refrigerated.

To cook the lamb chops, preheat oven to 375°F.

Remove the chops from the marinade and discard the marinade. Place the chops in a roasting pan. Roast the lamb chops for 15 to 20 minutes or until desired temperature is reached (125°F for rare, 130°F for medium rare).

Arrange the lamb chops on a platter, garnish with Fried Maui Onion Rings and serve.

Roasted Rack of Lamb
with Hawaiian Pepper Jelly

Pohā Chicken Skewers

Take this dish to your next picnic or potluck and it will be a hit. This recipe is based on Japanese yakitori or grilled skewers, popular in the islands. Always use the freshest and best chicken you can find. **Serves 4**

INGREDIENTS

4   pieces chicken breast, boneless
    and skinless, about 3 to 4 oz. each

12 6-inch bamboo skewers

    Salt and pepper to taste

Marinade:

½   cup pohā berry jam

¼   cup minced fresh ginger

¼   cup macadamia nut blossom honey
    or other honey

½   cup rice wine vinegar

½   cup canola oil

Garnishes:

4 ½-inch slices fresh pineapple

    Macadamia nuts, chopped

    Toasted white sesame seeds

    Toasted black sesame seeds

※

Cut each chicken breast into three strips on a sharp diagonal. Thread each strip onto a skewer. Season with salt and pepper.

In a blender, place the jam, ginger, honey and vinegar and blend at high speed until smooth, about 30 seconds. Slowly add the oil and blend until well mixed.

Pour half of the marinade over the chicken. Marinate, covered and refrigerated, for 3 to 4 hours or overnight. Cover and refrigerate remaining marinade.

To cook the chicken, preheat oven to 400°F. Place the chicken on a baking sheet. Bake the chicken in the oven until nicely browned and cooked through, about 6 to 8 minutes. Remove from the oven.

Arrange pineapple slices on four plates. Place chicken skewers upright in the pineapple slice. Drizzle with the remaining vinaigrette and sprinkle with macadamia nuts and white and black sesame seeds. Serve immediately.

Guava Spit Roasted Chicken

Now is the time to use that rotisserie on the barbecue or in the oven. But if you don't have one, oven roasting will work just as well to produce a moist, succulent and tasty chicken. **Serves 2**

In a small saucepan over medium heat, place the sauce, ginger, zest and chili paste. Simmer for 5 minutes. Remove from heat and cool. Season with salt and pepper to taste.

Place the chicken in a nonreactive bowl and pour ¾ cup of the sauce over. Marinate, covered and refrigerated, for at least 12 hours or overnight. Cover and refrigerate remaining sauce.

To cook the chicken, heat rotisserie. Remove the chicken from the sauce and discard sauce. Place the chicken on the rotisserie and slow roast for 45 minutes or until chicken is cooked (160°F on a thermometer). When the chicken is done, remove from the rotisserie and let rest for 10 minutes so the juices can redistribute into the meat.

Heat the remaining sauce. Cut the chicken in half down the center of the breastbone and back; separate legs from breast. Arrange pieces on two plates and drizzle with sauce. Garnish with cilantro and serve.

INGREDIENTS

1	whole chicken, about 3 lb.

Sauce:

1	cup guava grilling sauce
1	tsp. minced ginger
1	tsp. orange zest
1	tsp. sambal oelek or other garlic chili paste
	Salt and pepper to taste

Garnish:

	Fresh cilantro, chopped

Macadamia Nut Blossom Honey Mustard Chicken

Honey, mustard and apple wood smoked bacon are a perfect combination on chicken. This will become an instant favorite, especially if you serve it with roasted Yukon gold potatoes. **Serves 4**

INGREDIENTS

4	pieces chicken breast, boneless and skinless, about 3 to 4 oz. each
½	cup Italian dressing
¼	cup all-purpose flour
1	Tbsp. canola oil
4	slices bacon, chopped
½	Maui onion or other sweet onion, thinly sliced
1	tsp. fresh garlic, chopped
¼	cup Dijon mustard
¼	cup macadamia nut blossom honey
	Salt and pepper to taste
1	Tbsp. unsalted butter
4	slices mozzarella cheese, preferably buffalo mozzarella

Garnish:
Fresh parsley, chopped

In a small bowl, marinate the chicken in the Italian dressing. Cover and refrigerate for 3 to 4 hours or overnight.

To cook the chicken, remove from the marinade, drain well and discard marinade. Cut each chicken piece in half and lightly coat each piece with the flour. Heat a skillet over medium heat. When the skillet is hot, add the oil. Place the chicken in the pan and cook until both sides are golden brown and chicken is cooked through, about 6 to 8 minutes. When the chicken is cooked, remove from the pan and drain on a paper towel.

In the same pan over medium heat, add the bacon and cook until lightly browned. Add the onion and garlic and cook until onion is soft, about 3 minutes. Add the mustard and honey, stir to mix well and simmer for 1 to 2 minutes, adjusting heat to low. Season with salt and pepper to taste. Add the butter and stir in to blend.

Slice each chicken piece into diagonal strips and arrange on four warmed dinner plates. Spoon the sauce over the chicken. Place a slice of cheese on each portion; the heat from the sauce should melt the cheese. Garnish with parsley and serve.

Macadamia Nut Blossom Honey Mustard Chicken

INGREDIENTS

4   whole Cornish game hens

Marinade:

1   cup extra virgin olive oil

½   cup balsamic vinegar

½   Maui onion or other sweet onion,
      sliced thin

2   Tbsp. chopped fresh basil

1   tsp. salt

2   Tbsp. coarsely ground fresh black pepper

Stuffing:

½   lb. loaf sweet bread or other bread cut
      into 1-in. dice

1   Tbsp. canola oil

½   Maui onion or other sweet onion, diced

1   stalk celery, diced

1   tsp. chopped garlic

1   tsp. chopped fresh oregano

1   cup mango chutney

½   cup chicken stock

      Salt and pepper to taste

¼   cup chopped macadamia nuts

¼   cup unsalted butter, softened

Mango Chutney and Sweet Bread Stuffed Cornish Game Hens

Serves 4

Place the oil, vinegar, onion, basil, salt and pepper into a large bowl and whisk together until well mixed. Place the hens in the bowl and rub marinade into the skin and cavity. Cover and refrigerate for 3 to 4 hours or overnight.

To make the stuffing, preheat oven to 250°F. Place the bread on a baking sheet and bake in the oven until the bread has dried to a crisp and is golden brown in color. Remove from the oven and cool. Transfer to a large mixing bowl.

In a frying pan, heat the oil over medium heat. Sauté the onion, celery, garlic and oregano until onion is translucent, about 5 minutes. Add the chutney and chicken stock and simmer, stirring, until well mixed. Season to taste with salt and pepper.

Add the onion-chutney mixture to the bread and toss together. Add the nuts and butter and mix well.

To cook the hens, preheat oven to 300°F.

Remove the hens from the refrigerator and drain the marinade, discarding. Place the hens in a roasting pan and stuff each one with the stuffing. Roast the hens for 45 minutes or until cooked (160°F on a thermometer). Remove from oven and serve with additional mango chutney on the side.

Mango Chutney Thanksgiving Day Turkey

One of the best secrets to moist turkey is in this recipe: bone it, marinate it and then roast it to perfection. Turkey will never be the same again!

In a blender, place the olive oil, chutney, garlic, onion, rosemary, pepper, salt and paprika and blend at high speed until smooth, about 30 seconds. Transfer marinade into a large bowl. Dip each turkey piece into the marinade, coating well. Place pieces in one layer in a roasting pan with all of the marinade. Cover and refrigerate overnight.

To cook the turkey, preheat oven to 300°F. Remove the turkey from refrigerator and pour off the excess marinade, discarding. Bake the turkey for about 1 hour or until cooked (160°F on a thermometer). Remove the turkey from the oven and allow to rest for 5 minutes.

Slice the turkey and fan onto serving platter or individual plates. Garnish with mango and parsley and serve with more mango chutney alongside.

INGREDIENTS

1   whole turkey, about 12 to 14 lb., defrosted and deboned

Marinade:

2   cups extra virgin olive oil

½   cup mango chutney

2   Tbsp. minced garlic

1   Maui onion or other sweet onion, finely diced

1   Tbsp. finely chopped rosemary

1   Tbsp. coarsely ground black pepper

1   tsp. salt

2   Tbsp. paprika

Garnishes:

Fresh mango, finely diced

Fresh parsley, chopped

※

Guava Macadamia Nut Bread Pudding

Sweet Beginnings and Endings

Guava Waffles

For breakfast, waffles are a great treat. Top waffles with some guava or mango sorbet and it's a great dessert! For a variation, use passion fruit jelly in place of the guava syrup. **Makes 4 waffles**

Place the flour, baking powder, sugar and salt in a large bowl and mix.

In a separate bowl beat the eggs. Add the milk, guava syrup and butter and blend well. Add liquid mixture to the flour mixture, folding and mixing until smooth.

Heat a waffle iron and when it is hot, spray with a nonstick spray. Pour the batter into the center of the iron, leaving an inch around the edge. Close the iron and cook waffle about 4 to 5 minutes or until golden brown. Repeat with remaining batter.

Place waffles on heated plates and garnish with fresh fruit if desired. Serve with guava jam, guava strawberry jam or guava syrup.

INGREDIENTS

2	cups all-purpose flour
1	Tbsp. baking powder
2	Tbsp. sugar
1	tsp. salt
2	eggs
1½	cups milk
½	cup guava syrup (or passion fruit jelly)
¼	cup butter, melted

Guava French Toast with Moloka'i Sweet Bread

Portuguese sweet bread is legendary in Hawai'i: an egg and butter rich bread that makes great toast and French toast. When it comes from the island of Moloka'i, it's even more special. If you can't find sweet bread, a good quality thick sliced sandwich bread will be delicious, too. **Serves 4**

INGREDIENTS

8	slices Portuguese sweet bread
4	eggs
¼	cup milk
½	cup guava syrup
1	tsp. ground cinnamon
½	cup unsalted butter
	Confectioners' sugar for dusting

In a bowl, whisk together the eggs, milk, syrup and cinnamon until well blended.

In a large skillet over medium heat, melt 2 tablespoons of butter. Dip the bread in the egg mixture, coating well. Place the bread in the skillet and cook, browning each side. Remove from the pan and continue to cook remaining bread.

Cut each slice in half diagonally and arrange on plates. Dust with confectioners' sugar and serve with warm guava syrup on the side.

Macadamia Nut Blossom Honey Butter

INGREDIENTS

1	lb. unsalted butter, softened
½	cup macadamia nut blossom honey

This is a simple combination that can be used on pancakes, waffles, biscuits, muffins and plain old toast. Don't forget a steaming cup of Kona coffee alongside to start your day thinking about Hawai'i.

Place butter and honey in a food processor and blend until smooth. Cover and refrigerate until ready to use.

Guava French Toast with Moloka'i Sweet Bread

Pohā and Papaya Strudel

Pohā is the cape gooseberry, a golden green round berry that pops in your mouth with a distinctive tartness. Pohā berry jam is prized in the islands and offers an intriguing flavor to this classic dessert. **Serves 4**

INGREDIENTS

½	cup pohā jam
¼	cup macadamia nuts
8	sheets filo dough
1	cup (2 sticks) unsalted butter, melted
¼	cup granulated sugar
1	firm, ripe papaya, peeled, seeded and cut into 8 wedges

Garnishes:
Fresh strawberries, pureed
Fresh mango, pureed

✳

Preheat oven to 350°F.

In a small bowl, combine the pohā jam and macadamia nuts.

Lay 1 sheet of filo on a clean flat surface and brush with butter. Sprinkle with sugar and place another sheet of dough on top of it. Repeat until all the dough has been used.

Spread the pohā mixture along the length of the filo stack, leaving ½-inch at each end. Place the papaya on top of the pohā. Roll the dough up like a jellyroll, folding the ends in to seal. Place the roll on a baking sheet and brush the outside of the roll with butter. Bake in the oven until the filo is crisp and golden brown, about 15 to 20 minutes. Remove from the oven and cool.

To serve, slice the roll into eight pieces, discarding the ends. Place two slices on each of four plates. Garnish with strawberry and mango purees.

Guava Macadamia Nut Bread Pudding

Bread pudding is one of those classic, comfort desserts that everyone loves. It's a great way to use up leftover dinner rolls and bread. In this Hawaiian version, the flavor of guava, the perennial island favorite, makes this bread pudding a standout. **Serves 12**

Preheat oven to 375°F.

In a heavy bottom saucepan over medium heat, place the milk, guava jam, butter, vanilla, cinnamon and nutmeg. Whisk together and heat to a simmer. Remove from heat.

In a bowl, whisk together the egg yolks and sugar until smooth. Continue to whisk while slowly adding 1 cup of the milk mixture. Slowly whisk the egg-milk mixture back into the rest of the milk mixture.

Place the bread into a buttered 9 x13-inch baking dish and pour the milk mixture over the bread. Allow the bread to soak for 5 minutes. Place the baking pan in another pan and place in the oven. Fill the outer pan with hot water halfway. Bake until golden brown on top and a knife inserted in the center comes out clean, about 45 minutes.

To serve, cut the bread pudding into squares and place on individual plates. Dust with confectioners' sugar. Serve warm with ice cream or guava sorbet alongside.

INGREDIENTS

1	lb. bread, cut into 1-inch dice, toasted
3	cups milk, scalded
½	cup guava jam
¼	cup butter
1	tsp. pure vanilla extract
1	tsp. ground cinnamon
1	tsp. ground nutmeg
5	egg yolks
⅓	cup sugar
¼	cup confectioners' sugar, for garnish

※

Passion Fruit Crème Brulee

Crème brulee is everyone's favorite dessert – light, sweet, silky and scrumptiously delicious. In Hawai'i, tropical fruit flavors make this dessert especially wonderful. Here are two variations to fuel your dreams of paradise.

By the way, crème brulee does not require a blowtorch or special equipment to caramelize the top – your oven broiler will do the trick very well. **Serves 6**

INGREDIENTS

1¼ cups heavy whipping cream

1 cup passion fruit jelly

¼ cup coconut syrup

12 egg yolks

1 cup granulated sugar

1 tsp. vanilla extract

½ tsp. salt

Garnishes:

3 Tbsp. sugar

Fresh pineapple, finely diced

Papaya, peeled, seeded and thinly sliced

Toasted coconut flakes

✳

Preheat oven to 350°F.

Place the cream in a heavy bottomed saucepan over medium heat. Slowly bring the cream to a simmer. Add the jelly and coconut syrup and whisk until well blended. Bring the mixture back to a simmer and remove from the heat.

In a mixing bowl whisk together the egg yolks, sugar, vanilla and salt until the mixture is smooth. Slowly add the hot cream mixture to the egg yolk mixture, constantly whipping. Add the cream slowly so that the egg does not cook. When all the cream has been incorporated into the egg mixture, ladle the mixture into 6 crème brulee dishes or ramekins.

Place the dishes in a baking pan and place in the oven. Fill the pan with hot water, halfway up the sides of the dishes. Bake until the tops are golden brown and the crème brulee has set, about 15 to 20 minutes. To test for doneness, insert a knife into the center; the knife should come out clean. When cooked, remove the pan from oven, cool, cover and refrigerate until ready to serve.

To serve, heat oven broiler and position top rack near the heating element. Sprinkle ½ tablespoon of sugar over the top of each crème brulee. Place under the broiler for 30 to 60 seconds; sugar will melt and caramelize, turning a dark brown color. Remove immediately.

Place crème brulee dishes on individual plates and surround with pineapple and papaya. Sprinkle coconut over all and serve.

Passion Fruit Crème Brulee

Maui Pineapple and Papaya Crème Brulee

½ cup finely diced fresh pineapple

½ cup diced Maui papaya

1 cup Maui pineapple and papaya jam

¼ cup coconut syrup

1¼ cups heavy whipping cream

12 egg yolks

1 cup granulated sugar

1 tsp. vanilla extract

½ tsp. salt

Garnishes:

3 Tbsp. granulated sugar

Fresh pineapple, finely diced

Papaya, peeled, seeded and thinly sliced

Toasted coconut flakes

✳

Serves 6

Preheat oven to 350°F.

In a blender, place the pineapple, papaya, jam and coconut syrup and blend at high speed until smooth, about 30 seconds.

Place the cream in a heavy bottomed saucepan over medium heat. Slowly bring cream to a simmer. Add the fruit mixture and whisk together until well blended. Bring mixture back to a simmer and remove from heat.

In a mixing bowl whisk together the egg yolks, sugar, vanilla and salt until the mixture is smooth. Slowly add the hot cream mixture to the egg yolk mixture, constantly whipping. Add the cream slowly so that the egg does not cook. When all the cream has been incorporated into the egg mixture, ladle the mixture into 6 crème brulee dishes or ramekins.

Place the dishes in a baking pan and place in the oven. Fill the pan with hot water, halfway up the sides of the dishes. Bake until the tops are golden brown and the crème brulee has set, about 15 to 20 minutes. To test for doneness, insert a knife into the center; the knife should come out clean. When cooked, remove pan from oven, cool, cover and refrigerate until ready to serve.

To serve, heat oven broiler and position top rack near the heating element. Sprinkle ½ tablespoon of sugar over the top of each crème brulee. Place under the broiler for 30 to 60 seconds; sugar will melt and caramelize, turning a dark brown color. Remove immediately.

Place crème brulee dishes on individual plates and surround with pineapple and papaya. Sprinkle coconut over all and serve.

Guava Lemon Custard

A silky sweet and tart dessert, similar to a crème brulee but not quite. Serve this chilled on a hot summer night and you'll get rave reviews. **Serves 4**

In a saucepan over medium heat, place the cream, syrup, lemon zest and juice and bring to a simmer.

In the top of a double boiler set over simmering water, whisk the egg yolks and sugar until the mixture doubles in volume. Slowly pour the cream mixture into the egg mixture, whisking constantly. When all of the cream has been incorporated, continue to cook and stir the mixture until a thick custard forms, about 10 minutes. When the mixture is thick, ladle into ramekins or custard cups. Cool, cover and refrigerate until ready to serve, garnished with fresh fruit.

INGREDIENTS

1½ cups heavy cream

¼ cup guava syrup

Juice and zest of 1 lemon

5 egg yolks

1½ Tbsp. granulated sugar

Orange Mango Cobbler

There's nothing better than a cobbler when fresh fruit is in season. And when it's mango season in Hawai'i, cobblers are a special treat. **Serves 6**

INGREDIENTS

3	mangoes, half ripe, peeled, seeded and thinly sliced
1	Tbsp. ground cinnamon
¼	cup golden raisins
1	cup orange mango marmalade

Topping:

1	cup flour
1	tsp. ground cinnamon
½	cup brown sugar
1	cup unsalted butter, softened

✳

Preheat oven to 375°F.

In a large mixing bowl place the mango, cinnamon, raisins, and marmalade. Mix well and pour the mixture into a greased 10-inch pie pan or other baking dish.

In another bowl, mix together the flour, cinnamon, and sugar. With a pastry cutter or fork cut the butter into the flour mixture until crumbly and well mixed. Sprinkle the topping over the mango mixture. Bake until the topping is golden brown and the mango is tender, about 30 minutes.

Serve warm with macadamia nut ice cream or your favorite ice cream.

Tropical Sundaes

The simplest and one of the tastiest ways to enjoy the flavors of tropical island fruits is to serve them over ice cream. Make that macadamia nut ice cream for even more of the tropical theme.

In a saucepan over low heat, melt guava strawberry jam, pohā berry jam, pineapple and papaya jam or guava jam. Drizzle over scoops of ice cream and top with minced crystallized ginger, diced macadamia nuts and fresh chopped mint. Enjoy!

Tropical Sundaes

Mango Tatin

A tarte tatin is an upside down tart, usually made with apples. But in Hawai'i, mangoes reign supreme during the summer months and a mango tatin is a special treat. **Serves 6**

INGREDIENTS

3   ripe but firm mangoes, peeled,
    seeded and sliced

¾   cup brown sugar

1   tsp. ground cinnamon

¾   cup butter, melted

1½ cups mango chutney

6   3x3-inch puff pastry squares
    Confectioners' sugar for dusting

Preheat oven to 350°F.

In a large sauté pan over medium heat, sauté the mango, brown sugar and cinnamon with ½ cup of the butter. When the mango softens, about 3 to 5 minutes, add the chutney and simmer for 5 minutes. Remove from heat.

Brush some of the remaining butter into ramekins or crème brulee dishes. Divide mango mixture among the cups and top each with a piece of puff pastry. Brush the top of the puff pastry with the remaining butter. Bake until the pastry is golden brown, about 20 minutes. Remove from the oven and cool slightly. (At this point, the tart can be cooled and refrigerated until ready to serve. Tart can be reheated in a 300°F oven.)

To serve, loosen the edges of the tart using a small pairing knife. Flip the tart over onto a dessert plate. Dust with confectioners' sugar and serve with a scoop of vanilla bean ice cream.

Papaya & Pineapple Jam

Made in Hawai'i with Aloha

NET WT. 8 OZ (227G)

Guava Strawberry Jam

Made in Hawai'i with Aloha

Ingredients: Cane Sugar, Guava, Straw... Pectin, Citric Acid...

Refrigerate after opening

NET WT. 8 OZ (227G)

ingo
Made in Hawai'i

Glossary

Baby Greens: There is a wide variety of salad mixes today sometimes referred to as baby greens, mesclun or wild field greens. The contents of the mix will vary in texture and flavor, depending on the mix.

Black Beans: Fermented soybeans that are salty and pungent, used in Chinese cooking. It is often paired with garlic and ginger in fish and seafood dishes. To remove some of the saltiness, rinse or soak in water before chopping.

Bok Choy: One of many Asian cabbages, bok choy has white stems and dark green leaves. A baby version is sometimes available as well as Shanghai bok choy, a green stemmed variation.

Cajun Spice Seasoning: A blend of herbs, spices and chilies with its own unique flavor.

Chili Sauces: There is a wide variety of chili sauces available in Asian markets today. In this book, sambal oelek, a thin sauce of chilies, vinegar and garlic from Indonesia, and sweet Thai chili sauce, a thick red sauce of chilies, seeds, garlic, vinegar, salt and sugar, are used.

Chinese Five-Spice: A blend of five spices used in Chinese cooking. The spices are cinnamon, cloves, fennel, star anise and Szechuan peppercorns. The blend is widely available in markets.

Cilantro: Also known as coriander leaves or Chinese parsley, this flat leaf herb is used raw to add a distinctive flavor. It is widely used in Southeast Asian, Chinese, Mexican, Greek and Middle Eastern cuisines.

Lumpia Wrappers: Thin wheat flour and egg wrappers used in Filipino and Southeast Asian preparations. Available frozen in Asian markets.

Maui Onion: A sweet onion grown on the slopes of Haleakalā on the island of Maui. Substitute with Vidalias, Walla Wallas, Texas Sweets or other sweet onions.

Micro Greens:
Young shoots of salad greens and herbs, harvested when they are just an inch or two long and a few days old. They are packed with lots of flavor.

Panko:
Crisp bread flakes from Japan used as a coating for fried foods or a filler like bread crumbs. Available in Asian markets.

Pickled Ginger:
When ginger is young with a translucent skin and non-fibrous flesh, it is sliced very thin and pickled in seasoned vinegar. Also known as gari, it can be found in Japanese markets

Rice Vinegar:
A vinegar made from fermented rice, generally milder and slightly sweeter than distilled white vinegar. Substitute with white vinegar and adjust seasoning in recipe.

Sesame Oil:
Toasted sesame seeds are crushed to extract their oil, a dark, rich flavored oil used in Asian cooking.

Sesame Seeds:
White and black sesame seeds offer a distinctive flavor, especially if they are toasted. To toast sesame seeds, place them on a small baking sheet in a 300°F oven for about 5 minutes or until golden brown. Sesame seeds can also be toasted in a small skillet over medium heat.

Thai Red Curry Paste:
A blend of herbs and spices including lemon grass, garlic, ginger, cilantro, fish sauce and chilies. This thick paste is salty and spicy and is used by the spoonful as a base for Thai curry. It is available in Asian markets.

Wasabi:
Japanese green horseradish usually served with sashimi and sushi. There is limited availability of fresh wasabi in the U.S. Powdered and pureed wasabi found in markets are generally made of horseradish but are acceptable substitutes.

Island Plantations Jams & Jellies

Guava Strawberry Jam

Pink guava gets a flavor and color boost from strawberries, both grown on the island of Maui. With a little more depth of flavor, this jam will standout in many preparations.

Macadamia Nut Blossom Honey

Honey takes on the flavor of the blossoms that bees visit. In this case, Hawai'i's macadamia nuts provide the essence for this honey that is scrumptiously sweet and delicious.

Guava Jam

Everyone in Hawai'i grows up eating guava jam, the island favorite. Once found in the wild, cultivated guava is made into jam, syrup and juice. The sweet tart flavor of guava is unforgettable and so delicious!

Orange Mango Marmalade

Orange marmalade is a classic for toast and English muffins. But add the bright seductive flavor of mango and this marmalade will put you on a tropical island.

Pohā Berry Jam

Pohā, the cape gooseberry, grows on bushes in Hawai'i. This yellow green round fruit is like a small cherry tomato, but pohā has a tart, unique flavor unlike any other fruit. As a jam, pohā is prized in Hawai'i and can be used in many different preparations.

Passion Fruit Jelly

Passion fruit, also known as liliko'i, is an egg shaped fruit with a purple or yellow skin. Inside the soft pulp is orange with edible black seeds. This is a seductive sweet-tart tropical fruit with a pronounced perfume captured in this clear jelly.

Pineapple and Papaya Jam

Pineapple, the king of fruits, and papaya, creamy and melon-like, are two of Hawai'i's finest and most popular fruits. Blended into a jam, these tropical flavors are tantalizing.

Island Plantations Condiments

Coconut Syrup

This smooth, creamy and sweet coconut syrup embodies the Islands. The rich flavor of ripe coconut can be drizzled over fresh fruit such as bananas and pineapple, or poured over ice cream and sorbets. Top off breakfast favorites such as waffles and pancakes with the taste of the tropics, too.

Crushed Pineapple Syrup

The essence of field ripened pineapples, nourished by year-round sunshine, is captured in this syrup. Drizzle it over pancakes and waffles, use it as the flavor base for vinaigrettes and marinades. Only fresh pineapple beats this flavorful product.

Guava Syrup

The essence of guava can be drizzled over pancakes and waffles and especially ice cream and sorbets. Use a little in tropical drinks, too.

Guava Grilling Sauce

Guava's tropical flavor is highlighted in this sauce that can be used with anything you put on the grill. This is a must for ribs, chicken, steaks and fish.

Papaya Seed Dressing

The peppery edible seeds of papayas flavor this dressing. Use it over your favorite salad mix, as a marinade for poultry and fish or as a dipping sauce for fresh vegetables and fruit.

Island Plantations Condiments

Mango Chutney

When mango season begins in Hawai'i, it's mango chutney season. Green mangoes are simmered with herbs and seasonings to produce this flavorful condiment that enhances so many dishes. Just try some over cream cheese on a cracker!

Toasted Maui Onion Mustard

Maui onions are the sweetest on earth, nurtured on the slopes of Haleakalā on the island of Maui. Toasting the onions enhances its sweetness, creating a perfect balance for the pungent mustard. This will become your favorite mustard!

Maui Onion Salsa

Sweet Maui onions add their crunch to this flavorful salsa. Keep it handy for dipping with chips, topping a taco or grilled chicken and fish.

Hawaiian Pepper Jelly

Petite Hawaiian chili peppers are known for their fiery heat, captured in this jelly that is balanced with sweetness. It's the perfect glaze for hams, chicken and many more preparations.

ISLAND PLANTATIONS

To order call (800) 468-2800 or visit **islandplantations.com**